Country
by the Suss

From Thorney Island to Camber Sands

Jonny Young

Photographs by Jonny Young

S B Publications

BY THE SAME AUTHOR

Sussex Best Pub Walks: Arundel to Robertsbridge

First published in 2014 by S B Publications
Tel: 01323 893498
Email: sbpublications@tiscali.co.uk
Website: www.sbpublications.co.uk

ISBN 978-185770-371-9

Contents

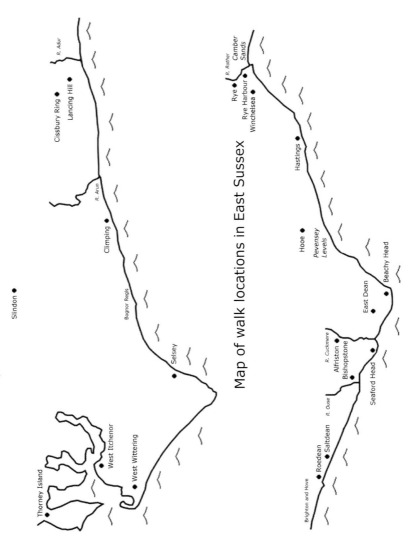

Map of walk locations in West Sussex

Map of walk locations in East Sussex

Introduction

At first glance, one could be forgiven for thinking that the coastline of Sussex might offer only pockets of interest to the countryside walker. Containing one of the most densely populated conurbations in the UK in the form of the ribbon of development between Brighton and Littlehampton, along with resort towns such as Eastbourne, Hastings and Bognor Regis, the landscape seems primarily urban, perhaps best enjoyed by strolls along the promenade.

However, well over half of the Sussex coastline has been designated a Site of Special Scientific Interest, from Chichester and Pagham Harbours in the west through to Pevensey Levels, Hastings Cliffs and Rye Bay in the east. It is these varied landscapes that the 20 walks in this collection explore: the shingle beaches at Climping and Rye, the cliff scenery at Beachy Head and Hastings and the sand dunes of West Wittering and Camber Sands which bookend the Sussex coastline.

Many have walked the 100-odd mile length of the Sussex shoreline, following its contours as closely as possible. This book aims rather to provide a selection of walks in the country that also give a flavour of a stretch of coastline, beginning at Thorney Island on the edge of West Sussex and ending some 75 miles east at Rye and Camber Sands in East Sussex. Occasionally, as at Slindon and Lancing Hill, the walks step inland so as not to compromise on the enjoyment of countryside, also allowing a greater appreciation of an expanse of coastline than might otherwise be possible.

Half of the walks in this collection lie within the South Downs National Park and a number also join long distance paths, such as the Sussex Border Path, South Downs Way, 1066 Country Walk, Saxon Shore Way and Monarch's Way, which provide much interest for further exploration.

All the walks are circular and range between 1.75 and 8 miles in length; they have been carefully described and tested in multiple seasons, although such is the changing nature of the countryside that use of the suggested Ordnance Survey maps is always recommended. The maps here are 1:25,000 scale.

The coastline which is visible from these walks has changed a great deal since the Romans arrived in Chichester shortly after AD 43, since the Normans arrived in Pevensey in 1066, and even since the threat of Napoleonic invasion was imminent in the early nineteenth century. Changes in sea levels have left some cliffs stranded some few miles inland, whilst some former villages now lie beneath the waves. Today, however, the present tidal mudflats, reclaimed marshland, sweeping bays, wooded valleys, chalk downland and sand dunes make for a diverse range of country strolls near the coast, as well as a rich variety of habitats for wildlife.

'Sussex by the Sea', that infectious tune heard at events from Lewes bonfire celebrations to Brighton and Hove Albion football matches, suggests how much the sea is entwined with the identity of the county. The countryside beside the Sussex coast is varied and vast, and it is hoped that the routes in this collection will provide an enjoyable glimpse into what it has to offer.

The Arun river estuary at Littlehampton

Thorney Island - Climping

The landscape of the Sussex coastal plain stretches from Chichester in the west across to Shoreham in the east, where the line of the South Downs begins to edge ever closer to the sea. Here, well-drained soils allow arable farming close to the shoreline, with many settlements having escaped the sprawl of urbanisation. Tidal inlets and mudflats near the natural harbours of Chichester and Pagham make ideal habitats for a variety of wildfowl such as plovers, sanderlings and dunlin.

The historical importance of Chichester Harbour is visible in Fishbourne, where evidence of buildings from the time of the first Roman invasion in 43 AD has been discovered. Nearby Bosham features on the Bayeux Tapestry as the site where last Saxon King Harold II set sail for Normandy.

Our walks visit the extreme west of the county at **Thorney Island**, the typical harbourside village of **West Itchenor** and the white sands of **West Wittering** at the mouth of Chichester Harbour. Moving eastwards, we explore the coastal inlets of Pagham Harbour via Church Norton and the shingle beaches near **Selsey**.

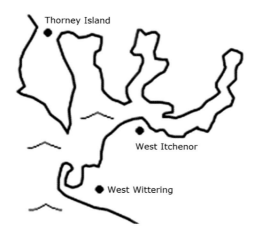

Coastline from Thorney Island to West Wittering

Not far away lies Bognor which, like West Itchenor, derives its name from being a Saxon landing place. The original village would later be developed into a seaside resort in the eighteenth century, following the trend set by Brighton thanks to Dr Richard Russell and the Prince Regent. In 1929, King George V would convalesce here, ultimately resulting in the suffix 'Regis' being added to its name.

Our route turns inland from Bognor Regis to the picturesque village of **Slindon**, allowing us the opportunity to appreciate the broad expanse of the coastal plain - much changed since prehistoric times when much of it would have been under water. Today, the ribbon of urban development is visible along the coast to the east, but at **Climping** it remains possible to stroll through arable farmland and woodland almost to the water's edge itself. The shingles along the beach here are, like those at West Wittering, popular haunts of oystercatchers.

Beyond Climping lies Littlehampton, known simply as Hampton until the fourteenth century. Here we reach the river Arun, the first of five major rivers which we will see draining into the sea along the Sussex coast. In 1835, the artist John Constable would paint one of his few Sussex works looking northwards from this estuary.

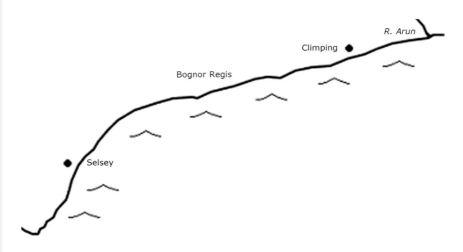

Coastline from Selsey to Climping

Thorney Island

F OR much of its history, Thorney Island was not in fact located in Sussex, and it was only from the latter half of the eighteenth century onwards that it stopped appearing on maps of Hampshire. Until the turn of the twentieth century it was an island in the true sense of the word, only accessible by a causeway that usually remained knee-deep in water even at low tide.

Today, Thorney Island is connected to the mainland, and our walk heads out along the seawall that now regulates the flow of the once perilous 'Great Deep'. Passing into property owned by the Ministry of Defence, in which the majority of our walk lies, we are then obliged to adhere to the only official path on the island.

This path skirts the perimeter of Thorney Island and runs almost exclusively along the shoreline, offering superb vistas across Chichester Harbour. The island itself is, owing to its lack of urban or agricultural use, a rich haven for wildlife, and at the southernmost point of the peninsula there are good views towards Pilsey Island RSPB reserve.

Looking across Emsworth Channel towards Hampshire

The walk: 7.5 miles

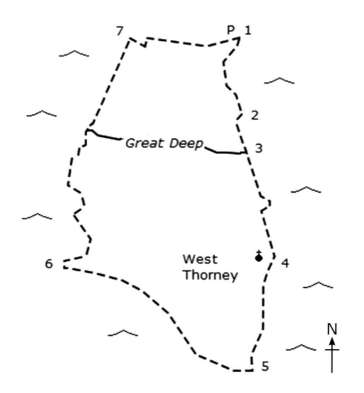

OS Explorer Map: 120 Chichester

Start: Car park at Prinsted, SU766051/PO10 8HS

Getting there: Via the A259 five miles west of
Chichester, following signs for Prinsted

Please note that because much of this walk lies within Ministry of Defence property, it is essential to stay on the marked path at all times.

1) Walk up the embankment towards the shoreline. The tarmac path along the seawall bears round to the left, whilst our route heads off to the right through a gate beside an information board for Nutbourne Marshes. Pass through the two boatyards of Paynes and Thornham Marinas, eventually emerging onto a raised levee at Thornham Point to be joined by a path from the right.

2) Follow the shoreline, first crossing a small oak bridge over a channel and then bearing right to meet a T-junction. Turn left over a stile and head along the top of the sea wall towards a tall security gate. Press the buzzer beside the gate and, if requested, give your name and address over the intercom. From here until point 7 the route lies within Ministry of Defence property, so it is important to stick to the marked path at all times.

Between 1938 and 1976, Thorney Island was used by the Royal Air Force, initially as a fighter station for aircraft involved with World War II. Today, the site is in the control of the Royal Artillery.

Nutbourne Marshes

Thorney Island - Climping

11

3) Continue along the narrow shoreline path, which eventually becomes a concrete track shortly before reaching a dinghy park. When this track reaches the sea, turn right up an embankment to reach a church.

Like many along the coast, this church is dedicated to St Nicholas, the patron saint of sailors. For much of its history it was one of the most remote churches in Sussex, since the parish in which it resides, West Thorney (named thus to distinguish it from East Thorney in Selsey, which has now been almost entirely lost to the sea), was not connected to the mainland by road until 1870.

4) Beyond St Nicholas' Church, the footpath joins a road beside a sailing club. Turn right and then very shortly left into the car park: signed 'High Water Footpath'. Keeping to the left, follow the path as it bears round behind the sailing club to return to the shoreline. Hugging the water's edge, the path eventually becomes hedge-lined before bearing right to reach the southernmost tip of the island.

Directly ahead are the dunes and mudflats of Pilsey Sands and the neighbouring area of Pilsey Island, an RSPB managed area which is a notable roosting site for migrating wading birds. In the distance, the mouth of Chichester Harbour opens

Pilsey Sands

out into the English Channel.

5) Shortly after Pilsey Sands, the path passes a bird hide before turning northwesterly, continuing to follow the shoreline on a broad track. After some two miles, this track forks at a Y-junction. Take the left-hand option, set between hedges, to soon reach memorial benches at Marker Point. From this point onwards, seals can sometimes be seen swimming in the channel on the west side of the island.

6) Beyond Marker Point, the path closely follows the contours of the shoreline to eventually reach another security gate. Press the buzzer and the guard will release the gate for you. On the other side of the security gate lies one mile of straight walking along the sea wall that regulates the flow of 'Great Deep'.

In 1870, the channel separating Thorney Island from the mainland was reclaimed for agriculture by constructing the two sea walls on which this walk passes. Today, the area is maintained as 178 acres of tidal mudflats and reedbed frequented by water rails, lapwings and grebes.

7) On the far side of the sea wall, the path reaches some distinctive black and white chalets on stilts. At a T-junction,

Hugging the shoreline beyond Marker Point

Thorney Island - Climping

turn right along a hedge-lined path and, just before some ramshackle buildings at Marina Farm, turn left up a steep bank and over a stile to emerge on the right hand edge of the chalet park. Almost immediately after a gravel track on the left, turn right over a stile between two yew trees. Cross directly opposite over a small field to reach Thorney Road.

8) Cross Thorney Road and follow the path along the right hand edge of, and soon on a raised bank between, a few small fields to reach a fenced pathway that runs along the left hand side of a house. Continue ahead down its gravel driveway to reach Prinsted Lane and turn left to return to the start.

Ministry of Defence signboard near St Nicholas' Church

West Itchenor

BORDERED on two sides by the creeks of Chichester Harbour, the village of West Itchenor has long had a history of maritime activity. It is likely that it would have had a role in providing boats for the ill-fated voyage of Harold II to Normandy that preceded the invasion of 1066, and today its sheltered waters house many pleasure craft.

Our walk begins in the village itself, whose name, like that of West Thorney, serves to remind of its one-time neighbour of which no trace remains. We head out beside the harbour's edge; across the inlet to the north lies Bosham, which counts both King Canute and Harold II among its former residents.

Turning inland across farmland, our route then passes the church and crosses towards the western side of the parish to follow the shoreline through woodland and reedbeds back to the village.

West Itchenor Harbour

The walk: 3.75 miles

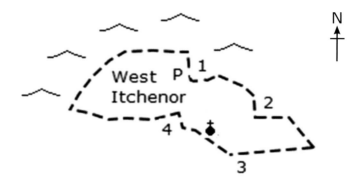

OS Explorer Map: 120 Chichester

Start: Car park at West Itchenor (fee paying), SU798012/PO20 7AH

Getting there: Via the A286 five miles southwest of the Chichester bypass, following signs for West Wittering and Itchenor

1) Leaving the car park entrance, follow the lane back to the main road through West Itchenor, The Street. Turn left and then shortly right down a road opposite The Ship Inn that leads towards Itchenor Sailing Club. The route soon passes along the edge of the harbour, eventually turning southwards on a narrow enclosed path to reach Spinney Lane.

2) Turn left and, at the end of the lane by The Spinney, turn right through a gate to pass along the left hand edge of a field with the harbour again visible on the left. At the end of the field, turn right to again walk along the left hand field edge with the hedge line to the left. Maintain direction on a clear grass path between two further fields to emerge by Oldhouse farm buildings.

3) Follow the drive down to a quiet road and turn right to pass a small village pond and church (dedicated, like many along the coast, to St Nicholas, the patron saint of sailors). When the road bears to the right soon after, continue straight ahead along a lane towards Itchenor Park House & Farm. Follow the route as it bears round to the right and to the left of a low wall beside the farm buildings and over a stile to reach a concrete drive.

Bosham Creek

Thorney Island – Climping

4) Turn left and maintain direction as the drive becomes a rough track. Deer can often be seen in the fields to the left. Eventually the route follows the left hand side of a field to reach the harbour. Turn right through woodland and reedbeds, following the shoreline edge back to West Itchenor. At a junction signed 'West Itchenor Permissive Path', a path on the right leads directly back to the car park.

West Itchenor village pond

West Wittering

L YING near the mouth of Chichester Harbour, West Wittering's golden sands are frequently featured in lists of the UK's best beaches. Our walk starts with a meander along the shoreline, enjoying the far-reaching views across the Solent to the Isle of Wight. At the end of the beach we reach East Head, an area of deposited shingle and sand formed by wind and wave action. In spite of being sheltered from some southwesterly winds by the Isle of Wight, the landform is constantly shifting due to wind and tide.

Skirting East Head, we then follow the edge of a tidal marsh on its lee side. Periodically flooded by both salt and fresh water, this fragile habitat sustains a multitude of invertebrates which provide food for many wading birds such as oystercatchers, little terns and curlews.

The latter part of our walk lies through woodland near the edge of Chichester Harbour, before heading by lanes to return to West Wittering beach.

Looking towards Hayling Island

The walk: 4.5 miles

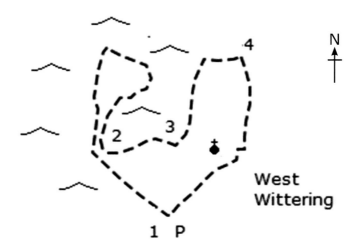

N

West
Wittering

OS Explorer Map: 120 Chichester

Start: Car park at West Wittering beach (fee paying),
SU780985/PO20 8AJ

Getting there: Via the A286 seven miles southwest of
the Chichester bypass, following signs for Bracklesham,
Witterings and West Wittering Beach

1) Walk down to the beach and turn right along the sand; ahead lies Hayling Island, while to the left the Isle of Wight is visible. Continue ahead towards the mouth of Chichester Harbour and bear right around the edge of East Head. Follow the beach as it doubles back around the spit, revealing a tidal salt marsh on the left.

East Head is a spit of shingle and sand dunes which is joined to the mainland by a narrow strip of sand known as the 'hinge'. Covering some 25 acres, this sensitive coastal habitat is now managed by the National Trust. Owing to the fragile nature of the dunes, access is permitted only via the duckboard paths.

2) Just before re-entering the beach car park, the footpath turns left along the sea wall. Soon after passing a crabbing pool, the path reaches the grassy area of Snowhill, from which the distinctive tower at Cakeham Manor, located on the site of a house owned by the Bishops of Chichester, can be glimpsed.

It has been suggested that this is the site of the first Roman landing in Sussex in AD 43. Later, it was used by smugglers: in 1743, 2000 lbs of tea were brought inland at West Wittering. Today, the salt marsh is frequented by waders

Sand dunes at East Head

Thorney Island – Climping

including redshanks, lapwings and curlews.

3) Continue to hug the harbour edge, passing a footpath on the right. Cross a slipway to a seat and ignore a second path away to the right, heading northwards beside open farmland and scrub. When the shoreline path eventually bears right beside a memorial seat, follow a tree-lined footpath.

4) On reaching a gate, turn right down Ella Nore Lane, passing Ella Nore Farm to reach Pound Road. Away to the left is The Studio, now a private house, on which a bronze plaque reveals that here some of Sir Henry Royce's greatest designs were carried out. Continue ahead, signed towards West Wittering Beach, following the footpath beside the road to return to the start point.

Looking northwards across the salt marsh towards Chichester

S TRETCHING just under a mile further into the English Channel than Beachy Head, Selsey Bill has the privilege of being Sussex's most southerly point. The name 'Selsey' is believed to derive from 'Seal Island', and the area remained surrounded by water on three sides until well into the eighteenth century. A large undeveloped natural harbour still exists to the north, offering the opportunity, particularly in autumn, to spot many migrating birds.

Our walk begins in Church Norton: the original location of Selsey. A chapel here lies on the site of an important cathedral from which St Wilfrid first introduced Christianity to pagan Sussex; this was destroyed by coastal erosion and the Normans would later relocate their ecclesiastical hub to the newly built Chichester Cathedral, the spire of which is visible from our path beside Pagham Harbour.

Due to its isolation, Selsey was a popular smugglers' haunt, although in the 1750s the authorities hanged two members of the infamous Hawkhurst Gang on gibbets on the tip of Selsey Bill to serve as a warning to others.

Towards Selsey Bill

The walk: 5.75 miles

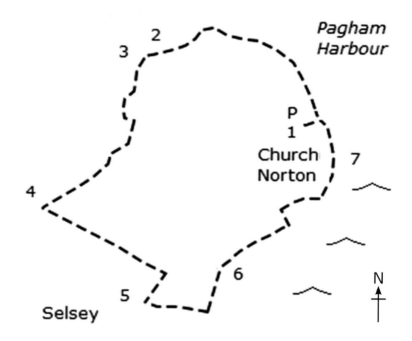

Pagham Harbour

Church Norton

Selsey

N

OS Explorer Map: 120: Chichester

Start: Car park at Church Norton, SZ871957/PO20 9DT

Getting there: Via the B2145 seven miles south of the Chichester bypass, following signs towards Selsey and then Church Norton

1) Leave the car park and walk to the right of a grassy mound marking the location of a former fort once protecting the entrance to Pagham Harbour. Pass a metal gate and an information board for Church Norton which denotes that this was the original settlement at Selsey before the resort grew out of the fishing community in the nineteenth century.

Soon the path reaches a T-junction by a saltmarsh and mudflats by another information board. This area is a haven for wading birds such as redshanks, curlews and godwits. Turn left to follow the edge of the harbour on boardwalks, shingle and then a raised embankment, passing a hide and then farmland on the left. Ahead, the spire of Chichester Cathedral can be seen.

The fields on the left mark the end of the southwest facing runway of the former RAF Selsey airfield, which was in use between May 1943 and May 1944 to support D-Day operations. A few miles to the north stands the site of RAF Tangmere (now the Tangmere Military Aviation Museum), one of the most familiar airfields of the Battle of Britain.

2) Shortly before reaching a main road, the path passes a bridge over Ferry Ponds/Broad Rife on the right; a bridge which used to carry the Selsey Tramway east of Pagham

Pagham Harbour

Thorney Island - Climping

harbour to Sidlesham and onward to its Chichester terminus some five miles to the north. At the point where the path itself begins to bear to the right and over Ferry Ponds Rife, continue ahead through a gap in the hedge to reach the road. A footpath sign confirms this as the route of the old Selsey Tramway.

Selsey Tramway ran between Chichester and Selsey Beach between 1897 and 1935. Designed by Colonel H. F. Stephens (who also built the Rye and Camber Tramway [see p. 111] and what is now known as the Kent & East Sussex Railway), it took some 30 minutes to complete the journey, which was made both by steam engines and hybrid petrol railbuses running on flanged wheels. Along its eight mile duration were no less than 11 stations, one of which, Ferry, stands a few yards from our current location and was the scene of regular collisions between trains and road vehicles. Eventually, train drivers had to walk across the road waving a red flag before the locomotive crossed.

3) Cross the road with care and, when the road bears left after a few yards, maintain direction through a metal farm gate. Head towards some ramshackle farm buildings, skirting to the right of these and then shortly back on to a track following the route of the old tramway. To the right, the Isle

Marker showing the route of the former Selsey Tramway

of Wight can be seen on a clear day. Follow the track as it skirts to the right of a hedgerow around the edge of Selsey Golf Club.

4) Ignore a turning to the right and, at a sign by a gap in the hedgerow immediately beyond some buildings for a country club, turn left. The path passes directly in front of the country club, shortly leading through a metal gate onto Golf Links Lane. Maintain direction, with a glimpse of Selsey windmill to the right. On reaching the main road, turn right.

5) Cross the road after 100 yards onto a clearly marked footpath opposite a police station. The path passes alongside the edge of houses, then around the right hand edge of a wild meadow and right down a tarmac path. Follow this over Manor Road (a few yards from where Selsey Town station would have stood) and continue to a second residential road, Manor Lane. Turn left and, when this bears round to the right, continue straight ahead on a rough track towards Park Farm.

6) Cross immediately opposite onto another track that skirts to the left of farm buildings and through the centre of fields. Eventually a sign guides the route left, following a line of trees along the left hand edge of a field. At the end of the field, veer away from the path straight ahead (leading to

View across the mouth of Pagham Harbour towards Bognor Regis

Thorney Island - Climping

Greenlease Farm) and turn right along the field's left hand edge towards the sea, passing a memorial and through woodland to emerge onto the beach.

7) Turn left at a series of large driftwood planks on the shingle beside the edge of Pagham Harbour to follow the path alongside the saltmarsh. A few yards away, the path rejoins the information board seen in point 1 and the route retraces its steps past the earthworks to Church Norton.

Looking northwards across Pagham Harbour to Chichester

D ESPITE being located some seven miles from the sea, Slindon nevertheless displays considerable 'coastal' interest. Half a million years ago this would have been the shoreline; nestling at the foot of the chalk dip-slope on which Slindon Wood now stands is a preserved shingle beach, suggesting that the sea level was once much higher than it is today. In 1994, a human shinbone was found at Boxgrove, a few miles to the west, which currently remains the oldest human fossil ever discovered in the UK.

Our route climbs up to Nore Folly, from which there is an excellent vantage point of the westward coastal plain, then through woodland to ultimately join Stane Street, the Roman Road linking Chichester and London. The downhill leg is predominantly through arable fields, with a glimpse to the eastward coastline, before returning through the attractive village of Slindon itself.

In autumn, tourists from across the country descend on Slindon to see the village's annual pumpkin display, something first started in 1968.

Downland above Slindon

The walk: 7 miles

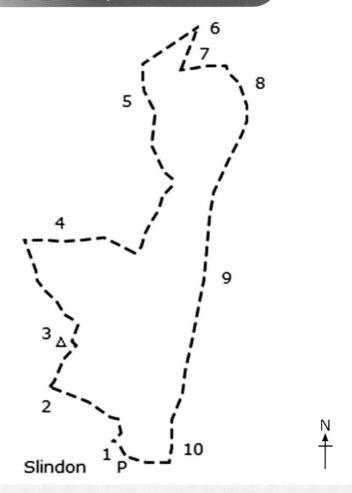

OS Explorer Map: 121 Arundel & Pulborough

Start: Top Road, Slindon, SU961084/BN18 0RH

Getting there: Via the A27 or the A29 five miles west of Arundel

1) Facing away from the village, follow the road as it curves round past the entrance to Slindon College (originally a manor house) and shortly turn right on a lane heading downhill. When this begins to bear round to the right beside Courthill Farm, turn left onto a track which climbs gently between fields.

2) Just before a lone flint wall at Row's Barn, turn right onto a track that heads uphill along the right hand side of fields towards the clearly visible gateway structure of Nore Folly. On the left, the round cap of Halnaker Mill, a windmill which lends its name to a poem by Hilaire Belloc, can be seen.

From Nore Folly there are panoramic views back towards the coastline at Bognor Regis, the spire of Chichester Cathedral and across to the Isle of Wight. Many thousands of years ago, most of the area ahead would have been flooded and the shoreline would have lain less than a mile away.

3) The path continues up Nore Hill past the folly, shortly bearing left into woodland through a metal gate beside a sign reading 'Warning Forestry Operations'. Follow the path through the woodland and turn right at a fork. At a second fork, continue ahead downhill to reach a T-junction and turn right. In summer, there are attractive displays of the rare

Trig point below Nore Folly

Thorney Island - Climping

deep pink pyramidal orchid along this stretch of the walk.

4) On reaching a cross-path at the edge of the wood, continue straight ahead along a track beside a large arable field to shortly reach a second cross-path. Turn left on a wide half-made track to head uphill, passing the distinctive tiled roof of Ware Barn. Eventually the track passes through a double wooden gate and straight ahead through Gumber Farm.

Run by the National Trust, Gumber Farm and Bothy now offer a secluded spot for campers. In World War II, a dummy airfield was laid out here, and this area of Sussex was also much praised in the writing of Hilaire Belloc.

5) Head through three further sets of gates and then, at a T-junction shortly after, turn right onto Stane Street: a distinctive banked path made by the Romans for use as the main transport artery between Chichester and London.

6) Ignore the first turning on the right but take the second, heading diagonally right downhill and keeping to the right of a few isolated trees in the middle of the field. The spire of Chichester Cathedral is visible on the right.

Gumber

7) Head through a gate to join a cross track and turn left, continuing ahead at a junction that crosses the small valley of Great Bottom. As the way enters woodland, bear right away from the track. The path heads right, through the woodland, and soon joins a path entering from the left.

8) Turn right, heading downhill. At a fork, keep left to soon reach a wide wooden gate on the edge of the woodland. Maintain direction across the centre of a large field, with the coastline panorama clearly visible, reaching a second gate and then heading through the centre of two arable fields.

9) On meeting a cross junction at the end of the second of these two fields, continue ahead through woodland on a path which soon becomes a track offering excellent views eastwards. Soon, this emerges into Slindon on the corner of Baycombe Road and Mill Lane.

10) Continue ahead down Mill Lane, passing the old village pound, to reach a road junction. Turn right, opposite a bakery, and follow the road past the former house of the writer and poet Hilaire Belloc.

IN 1903
BLEAK HOUSE
BECAME THE FIRST
SUSSEX FAMILY HOME
OF

HILAIRE BELLOC

1870 ─ 1953

WRITER AND POET
AND HIS WIFE
ELODIE

WEST SUSSEX COUNTY COUNCIL

Plaque on the former house of Hilaire Belloc

Thorney Island – Climping

After passing Slindon Pottery and a farm from which creative pumpkin displays can be seen in autumn, continue over a small roundabout to return to Slindon College.

Hilaire Belloc spent much of his childhood in Slindon, returning to live in the village in 1903 before later moving to Shipley, where he remained till the end of his life. Much of his writing praises Sussex, in particular the western South Downs.

Top Road, Slindon

Climping

MUCH of the farmland we explore near Climping would once have been part of the Arun river estuary. The original mouth of the river, which rises near Horsham, is thought to have been further southwest of its present location; longshore drift caused it to be deflected ever eastwards until its current course was artificially cut in 1735.

This part of the Sussex coast has long suffered from erosion, with most of the settlements of Atherington and Cudlow being lost to the sea by the late seventeenth century. Today, a sand dune ecosystem which we visit beside the western embankment of the Arun is protected as a Site of Special Scientific Interest and managed as part of the West Beach Local Nature Reserve.

To the west of Climping lies Felpham, where William Blake wrote his poem 'Milton', best known for its famous lines praising 'England's green and pleasant land'; lines that would later become the hymn 'Jerusalem'. Fittingly, the composer Sir Hubert Parry, who set the music to 'Jerusalem' in 1916, made his home in nearby Rustington.

Sand dunes at West Beach, Littlehampton

The walk: 4.5 miles

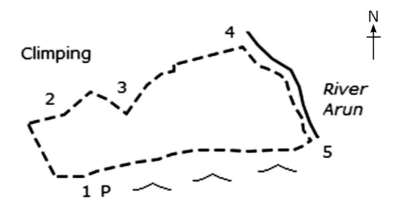

OS Explorer Map: 121 Arundel & Pulborough

Start: Car park at Climping Beach, TQ007008/ BN17 5RW

Getting there: Via the A259 two miles west of Littlehampton, following signs for Climping Beach and Bailiffscourt Hotel

1) Follow the road out of the car park, curving right to pass the entrance to Bailiffscourt Hotel on the left. Shortly after reaching the Black Horse Inn, turn right along a track beside a few thatched cottages. When this bears round to the left, maintain direction by striking out across the centre of a field towards a junction with a public byway.

2) Continue on the footpath, heading half-left towards a distinctive red-roofed building. When the path leaves the field, turn immediately right opposite a flint wall onto a path that skirts around the field edge and into the farmland beyond, following a boundary hedge. When the hedge line on the left ends, head diagonally right to cross a concrete footbridge in the field's far corner.

3) Turn left by a footpath sign to follow the line of a channel known as the Ryebank Rife, one of many channels dug to drain the area for agricultural use. On reaching a second footpath sign, head half-right towards a telegraph pole in the field corner beside a line of trees. A further footpath sign leads the route beside a second drainage channel and over a small footbridge to reach Ferry Road. Cross the road and turn right.

Cottages near Climping Street

Ahead, a bridge crosses the river Arun; between 1824 and 1908, there was a chain ferry here, giving rise to the road's name. Until the construction of this road, it would only have been possible for the villagers of Climping to travel to Littlehampton at low tide using the exposed ridges of sand at the mouth of the river.

4) Just before reaching the bridge, turn right down a road signed towards Arun Yacht Club and Littlehampton Golf Club, shortly veering left beside a sign marked 'Public footpath to West Beach ½ mile'. Follow the path beside the river Arun, passing Arun and Littlehampton Yacht Clubs to reach West Beach.

5) Turn right beside a sign marked towards the visitor centre, following the boardwalks through West Beach Sand Dunes. Away to the right, amidst this managed sand dune system, are traces of a fort built in 1854 to defend Littlehampton harbour against the threat of Napoleonic invasion; strengthening of the banks of the river Arun has prevented the natural spread of the dunes eastwards and allowed them to build up at this point. When the boardwalk emerges onto the beach itself, turn right, following the beach back towards the car park in Climping.

Looking towards Climping Beach

Cissbury Ring - Saltdean

Beyond Littlehampton lies one of the largest conurbations in the UK, a ribbon of urban development which continues almost unabated for some 20 miles to reach Brighton Marina, encompassing smaller settlements such as Rustington, Preston, Angmering, Kingston and Goring.

Above Worthing, where writers Harold Pinter, Oscar Wilde and Jane Austen would respectively live, holiday and convalesce, our course steps northwards to **Cissbury Ring**. From this ancient hill fort site there is an expansive panorama over the shallow inward curve of this stretch of coastline as it arcs towards Brighton and beyond.

East of Cissbury Ring, overlooking the river Adur, lies **Lancing Hill**. The walk here allows an appreciation of the Adur estuary and the settlement of Shoreham, which rose to prominence as a port in the early Middle Ages. Much of the original town was destroyed by rising sea levels in the fourteenth century, though the new town was to develop a thriving shipbuilding industry. The building of wooden ships ceased by the end of the nineteenth century and the industry went into decline, although in the early twentieth century one of the country's

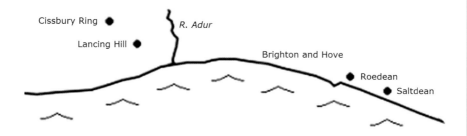

Coastline from Cissbury Ring to Saltdean

first airports was established here, as well as Sir Harry Ricardo's automobile business.

After Shoreham and Southwick, West Sussex gives way to the unitary authority of Brighton and Hove. Developed from a humble fishing settlement in part by Dr Richard Russell's popularising of the sea as a remedy for almost all ailments, Brighton's popularity was improved by the Prince Regent's patronage and, with the advent of the railway, by its proximity to London. Having possessed three piers over its history, the town is a temple to leisure: made famous in the opening scenes of Graham Greene's 'Brighton Rock'.

East of Brighton, the coastal landscape changes dramatically. The chalk cliffs for which the Sussex coastline is perhaps most famous begin to dominate, rising above Madeira Drive – best known as the finish line for many London to Brighton car and cycle runs. This area of the coast is characterised by a number of 'denes', or valleys, which nestle in the dips of these undulating cliffs. We visit four of these – **Roedean**, Ovingdean, Rottingdean and **Saltdean** – crossing downland and following the sea wall at the foot of the cliffs. At Saltdean, we move into East Sussex, after which lies Peacehaven, where the Sussex coastline is dissected by the Greenwich Meridian.

Above Telscombe Village

Cissbury Ring

S ET back from Worthing, the downland summit of Cissbury Ring affords spectacular views over an area of coastline normally considered as a ribbon of urban development. Chosen as an appropriate site for an Iron Age settlement between the fifth and first century BC, Cissbury Ring was one of the UK's largest hill forts – its mile-long defensive boundary walls surrounding some 60 acres. It also had one of the highest concentrations of flint mining in the country, with several mines providing weapons and tools that would have been transported over the downland far and wide.

A mile to the north of our walk lies the Monarch's Way, a 615 mile long distance footpath that runs from Worcester to Brighton and then back to Shoreham along the approximate route taken by Charles II following his defeat by Oliver Cromwell in the Battle of Worcester in 1651, after which he would spend the next nine years in exile until the restoration of the monarchy in 1660.

Below Cissbury Ring

The walk: 1.75 miles

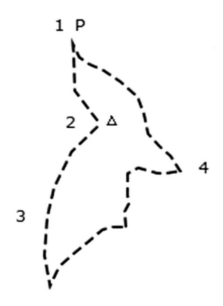

N

OS Explorer Map: 121 Arundel & Pulborough

Start: Car park at Cissbury Ring, TQ139085/BN14 0SQ

Getting there: From the A24 five miles north of Worthing, follow signs for Findon or Nepcote and then towards Cissbury Ring

1) Follow a broad chalk track uphill past an information board. When the track begins to curve round to the left, continue straight ahead through a kissing gate and climb a number of staggered steps leading to one of the ditches that mark the outer ramparts of this former fortification. Crossing the ditch, continue up a further series of smaller steps and then head directly uphill towards a series of low shrubs, with a trig point soon coming into view.

On a clear day, there is an excellent view eastwards from this trig point towards Shoreham, Brighton and beyond as far as Seaford Head.

2) Facing the trig point and continuing to look eastwards, turn right on a grassy path lined with gorse bushes to head downhill in the direction of the coast. The path soon opens out as it heads through the centre of the old settlement, revealing a larger panorama of the coastline. Undulations underfoot are the only surface indications of the myriad flint mines that once supported a thriving industry here. Continue directly ahead, passing between two raised banks and over another ditch marking the fort's southern boundary.

3) Almost immediately after crossing another ditch, pass through a kissing gate and continue downhill on a chalk track

Shoreham Bay

Cissbury Ring – Saltdean

through light woodland to reach a signed junction. Ahead lies Worthing, while away to the right is the village of Findon. Take the path signed towards Steyning Bowl, turning left on a chalk track beside a metal field gate which winds downhill.

The village of Findon is renowned for its traditional sheep fair, which takes place each September. An annual fair has been held here as long ago as 1261 and, although sheep auctions no longer take place at the event, there remain sheep displays which still include the traditional Sussex Southdown breed.

4) When the track curves back uphill to reach a T-junction, turn left and soon pass through a wooden gate to the left of a metal field gate. On the right, the distinctive radio masts at Truleigh Hill can be seen as the track winds downhill back to the start.

Worthing coastline as seen from Vineyard Hill below Cissbury Ring

Lancing Hill

V IEWED from the hills above Lancing, the panorama over the shallow inward curve of Shoreham Bay is clearly appreciable. The River Adur cuts through the downland to make its estuary at this point and it is easy to see why Shoreham's natural geography and relative proximity to both London and Normandy enabled it to develop rapidly as a port during the medieval period.

Indeed, until the late nineteenth century, Shoreham was one of the most important points along the Sussex coast: the decline in the use of wood in shipbuilding had a deep impact on the resort's prominence. In 1911 Shoreham Airport was opened, making it one of the oldest airports in the UK; its founding flight was a few hundred yards to the north, reaching roughly where the Sussex Pad inn lies along the A27 today. Interestingly, there is evidence of a former beach at this point, revealing the fluctuations in sea levels over numbers of years.

View towards Shoreham and the Adur river estuary

The walk: *4.25 miles*

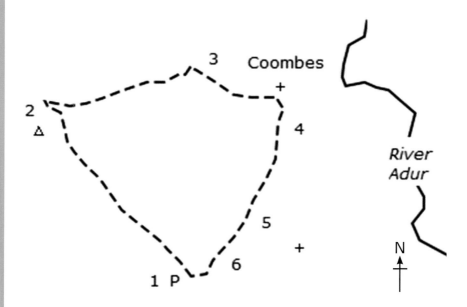

OS Explorer Map: 122 Brighton & Hove

Start: Car park at Lancing Ring, TQ183062/BN15 0QD

Getting there: From the A259 two miles west of Shoreham, follow signs for North Lancing, Manor Road and Mill Road

1) Leaving the car park, turn left to follow the track uphill. This passes woodland, then to the right of the broad expanse of Lancing Ring Nature Reserve, above which skylarks are often heard in summer. Follow a well-worn track towards and round the right hand edge of the hill brow ahead. Behind, Worthing stretches out below, with the view stretching as far as Beachy Head in the east on a clear day.

2) When the track eventually begins to descend, pass beneath a large pylon and then almost immediately turn right through a wooden gate situated to the right of a metal field gate. Follow the top edge of a steeply sloping field, aiming for a clump of trees on the top of the brow of the hill ahead. Continue to follow the right hand fence line past the clump of trees as the Adur estuary and Shoreham Harbour come into view. Below, bounded by river, downland and sea, lies the airfield at Shoreham Airport.

3) Pass through a gate beside a cattle grid and continue to follow the right hand fence line, heading away from a track on the left that leads down into Coombes. When the path joins with a track at a junction above Coombes, turn right through a small wooden gate and turn immediately right to follow the right hand edge of fields. The distinctive structure of Lancing College Chapel, whose ceiling stands 94 feet high (making it

Track east of Lancing Ring Nature Reserve

one of the tallest church interiors in the country), is visible presiding over the Adur valley.

4) Pass over a stile and onto an enclosed track between fields. Go through a wide kissing gate and head downhill, passing through a second kissing gate and over a concrete drive to descend into the valley of Cowbottom.

5) At the bottom of the valley, pass a large pound, cross a stile and then follow an enclosed path that heads steeply uphill. Cross another stile at the top of the hill and head directly ahead through the centre of a large arable field, with Shoreham airfield and the shoreline beyond coming into view.

6) On the other side of the field, pass through a gate to head through a very short valley and over a stile to join a track heading uphill. Turn right, and the car park is very shortly visible on the left.

Looking eastwards from Lancing Hill

E AST of Brighton, the coastline begins to be dominated by the exposed chalk cliffs for which Sussex is renowned. Beyond Brighton Marina, an undercliff walk allows us to traverse the sea wall which was built in the 1930s to slow erosion, and which is continually being reinforced. When the tide is out, it is just possible to see the concrete foundations of Magnus Volk's attempted offshore Brighton and Rottingdean Seashore Electric Railway.

Magnus Volk, best known to Brighton residents as the founder of the Volk's Electric Railway (suggested to be the world's oldest electric railway still in existence today) which runs just west of Brighton Marina to the Aquarium, is buried in nearby Ovingdean, one of a number of former agricultural communities nestling in the valleys near this area of coastline.

We begin, however, in Roedean, by a famous independent girls' boarding school boasting many notable alumni – including some who are fictional.

Ovingdean coastline

The walk: 5 miles

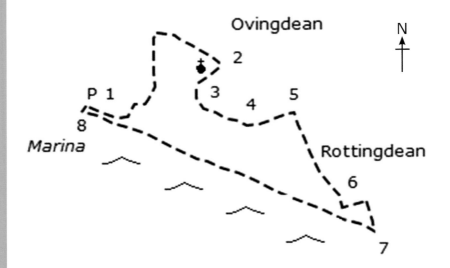

OS Explorer Map: 122 Brighton & Hove

Start: Car park at Roedean, TQ347031/BN2 5RQ

Getting there: Via the A259 three miles east of Brighton centre

1) Heading away from the sea, pass the entrance to Roedean School and follow a fingerpost signed 'Ovingdean 1¼ miles' to skirt the right hand side of a sloping field. Over the brow of the hill, Woodingdean comes into view as the path becomes a chalk track bearing right, shortly being joined by two paths from the left. Soon, the track passes beside buildings at Bulstrode Farm to join Greenways, the main road through Ovingdean.

2) Maintain direction, turning right by a footpath sign towards Ovingdean church. Immediately to the right of the churchyard gate, cross a stile to follow a flint wall beside the edge of the churchyard to reach a second stile in the left hand corner of a small field.

3) Continue ahead, climbing steeply for a few yards to reach the top of the hill. Immediately before a stile, turn right to walk downhill; from this vantage point, it is possible to see as far as Shoreham and Worthing. Follow the fence line as it guides the path eastwards, with the windmill on Beacon Hill visible ahead.

4) Shortly before reaching the bottom corner of the field, pass through a gate on the right and maintain direction, this time along the left hand side of the field beyond. Pass through

Beacon Hill Nature Reserve

Cissbury Ring - Saltdean

two further gates to re-join Greenways. Cross straight over the road and onto Beacon Hill.

5) When the road bears round to the left, turn right and pass an information board for Beacon Hill Nature Reserve. Head through a gate and go straight ahead along the top of the hill, along the wider of the two possible tracks. Shortly after passing directly beside the windmill, head through another wooden gate to leave Beacon Hill.

6) Continue ahead along a tarmac drive to reach a residential road. Turn left to soon pass a sign reading 'Caution Steep Footpath'. Walk down this with care to reach Rottingdean High Street. Turn right through the village and cross over the main road, passing the White Horse pub to reach the sea.

7) Turn right and follow the path along the seawall beneath the undercliff. This easy stretch of walking is very popular with locals and continues for just under 1½ miles to reach Brighton Marina.

8) At the marina, follow the tarmac path to the top of the cliff, from the top of which it is possible to see the distinctive piers of Brighton. Walk up to the main road and cross with care. Turn right for a few hundred yards to cross Roedean Road and return to the start point.

Rottingdean and Beacon Hill windmill

A LTHOUGH the area occupied by Saltdean and nearby Peacehaven has been shown to have been inhabited thousands of years ago, the landscape consisted of farmland for most of its history. It was not until the 1920s, when the farmland was sold off to speculative builders, that these two seaside resorts were created in their current forms.

Our walk begins close to the famous 1930s Art Deco lido in Saltdean before heading along the undercliff walk towards Rottingdean, where Rudyard Kipling made his home between 1897 and 1902. At the time, Kipling's uncle, the Pre-Raphaelite painter Edward Burne-Jones, lived in the village, with his cousin, future Prime Minister Stanley Baldwin, a regular visitor.

Striking out towards the Downs, we skirt behind Saltdean and head towards Telscombe Village. A little way east lies Peacehaven, home to a cliff top monument marking the southernmost point on which the Greenwich meridian lies on UK soil.

Undercliff walk between Saltdean and Rottingdean

The walk: 7 miles

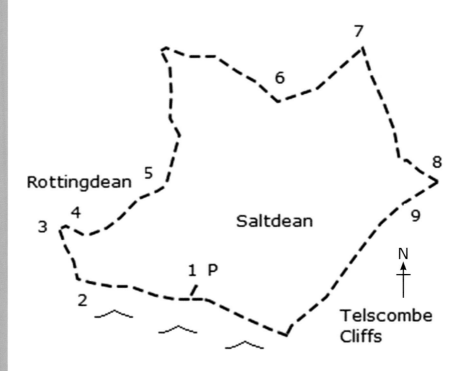

Rottingdean

Saltdean

Telscombe Cliffs

N

OS Explorer Map: 122 Brighton & Hove

Start: Car park by Saltdean Lido, TQ382021/BN2 8SP

Getting there: Via the A259 five miles east of Brighton, following Saltdean Park Road

1) Follow Saltdean Park Road towards the seafront, passing Saltdean Lido. Almost immediately before reaching the main coast road, turn right onto a sloping surfaced path which leads under the road to emerge by the beach; on the left, it is just possible to glimpse Seaford Head. Turn right along the undercliff walk, a path along the top of the defensive sea wall that runs at the foot of the cliffs between Saltdean and Brighton Marina.

2) After some three-quarters of a mile, the path is joined by a broad slipway from Rottingdean. Turn right up this, passing The White Horse. On reaching traffic lights beside a junction with the main coast road, cross straight ahead to follow the High Street into Rottingdean village. Maintain direction, eventually passing St Martha's Convent to reach the village green. A short way away on the left is the white-walled Prospect Cottage, on which is a blue plaque dedicated to the painter Edward Burne-Jones.

3) Turn right immediately opposite North End House towards an information board for Kipling Gardens. Our route skirts the outer wall of the gardens, passing in front of The Elms – the residence which Rudyard Kipling rented for a time until 1902, when he would move to Bateman's, near Burwash.

Village pond at Rottingdean

Cissbury Ring – Saltdean

4) On the opposite side of the green, turn right to pass the village pond. Beyond this, by the Plough Inn, cross onto Whiteway Lane with The Grange Art Gallery and Museum to its left. Continue ahead as the lane narrows into an unmade track and, when this forks, take the left hand option. Maintain direction as the track is joined by another from the left to emerge at the end of a residential road in Saltdean.

5) Turn left on a public bridleway signed towards Woodingdean. Briefly passing between houses, the track then heads out into downland, offering a broad view back over to the Rottingdean coastline and Roedean School. Continue ahead through a gate and along the left hand edge of a large arable field. At the end of this, turn right immediately before another gate to follow the field edge downhill.

In the valley ahead lies the deserted hamlet of Balsdean. Owing to its remote location, the population of the settlement was evacuated in the Second World War and the buildings used for target practice. After the war, the buildings were never rebuilt and the villagers never returned.

6) In the bottom of the valley, the path reaches Pickers Hill Farm and joins a concrete track by farm buildings to meet a fingerpost. Take the left hand option, climbing uphill on a

Rottingdean viewed from the downland behind Saltdean

broad track alongside an arable field with a hedgerow on the right. Follow the track as it continues northwards, passing into a further field.

7) On meeting a footpath junction at the top of the hill, turn right through a metal gate. Maintain direction along the hilltop, from which there are excellent views back into the Saltdean valley. After passing a small reservoir on the right, pass through a gate and walk along the edge of a field above the tiny settlement of Telscombe Village. At the end of the field, head through two gates in quick succession to join a gravel track with views over the coastline towards Peacehaven.

8) When the gravel track meets a lane above Telscombe Village, turn right on path marked as a public right of way. Very soon this splits; take the right hand option leading down the western side of Telscombe Tye with Peacehaven stretching out along the cliff top away to the left.

Telscombe Tye is an area of common land (the word 'Tye' derives from the Old English for 'common') that separates Saltdean from Peacehaven and Telscombe Cliffs. In the 1930s Ambrose Gorham, Lord of Telscombe Manor, refused to sell the land for construction and the area has remained

Telscombe Village

Cissbury Ring – Saltdean

undeveloped since. During 1916-19 an airfield to the east was involved in anti-submarine patrols supporting a seaplane station operating in Newhaven at the same time; in happier times, pleasure flights were offered from the Tye in the 1930s.

9) Follow the track, an ancient highway popular with smugglers carrying contraband from Saltdean beach, to eventually reach the foot of the Tye and head through a gate to meet the main coast road. Cross with extreme care and turn right along the clifftop. Head downhill for a few hundred yards to return to Saltdean and turn right onto Saltdean Park Road to return to the start point.

Looking towards Saltdean

Bishopstone - Beachy Head

The stretch of coastline east of Brighton is broken by the River Ouse as it meets the sea at Newhaven. A village had existed here since the Saxon era, and evidence of earlier defences have been found on Castle Hill (where Newhaven Fort now stands), but at the time, the river meandered to its estuary in Seaford. The impact of longshore drift and storms resulted in the cut being made in its present location, and the development of the town as it is today.

Our first walk in this section begins in **Bishopstone**, an attractive village which would have been strategically sheltered from this once marshy tidal estuary. We briefly step inland to **Alfriston**, where there is a panorama over the coastline between Newhaven and Cuckmere Haven, before visiting three Sussex icons: **Seaford Head**, **East Dean and the Seven Sisters** and **Beachy Head**.

Seaford, whose situation as a port was made redundant by the shifting location of the Ouse, is home to the most westerly Martello tower built in southeast England: one of the 47 round fortresses built in Sussex in the eighteenth century to protect

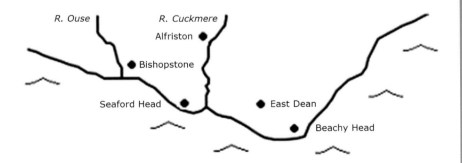

Coastline from Bishopstone to Beachy Head

the coast against the perceived threat of Napoleonic invasion.

Beyond Seaford Head we reach the unspoiled Cuckmere estuary, exploring both sides of the river valley. We join one arm of the South Downs Way which has split east of Alfriston: the footpath-only section veering southwards towards the sea, where we pick it up on two classic walks over the Seven Sisters and Beachy Head.

Formed millions of years ago, these cliffs between Seaford Head and Beachy Head have proved treacherous for many sailors; at low tide it is still possible to glimpse the wrecks of one or two near Cuckmere Haven and Birling Gap.

Today, the cliffs are eroded at a rate of up to 15 inches every year, with the cottages at Birling Gap in danger of being lost to the sea and the clifftop lighthouse at Belle Tout having already once been moved some 50 feet inland.

Our final stretch of chalk downland in Sussex, and the most westerly extent of the South Downs National Park, lies at Beachy Head, the highest chalk sea cliff in the UK and one of the most southerly points in Sussex. Indeed, neighbouring Eastbourne consistently lays claim to being one of the sunniest places in the country.

Looking westwards from Beachy Head

BISHOPSTONE possesses a church believed to have been built between 700 and 800 AD, making it one of the oldest in the county. The settlement itself lies behind the former floodplain between Newhaven and Seaford at the most northerly point of a one-time tidal inlet (walkers arriving by public transport will follow the site of this to reach the start point).

In the Middle Ages, the River Ouse meandered east of its current route to meet the sea at Seaford, with a combination of storms and longshore drift causing frequent flooding upstream on the land in front of Rookery Hill, which we ascend at the beginning of our walk. Indeed our return to the village joins the medieval route from Bishopstone to East Blatchington and Seaford which would have avoided the marshy land by the Ouse estuary.

Today, the village lies some way inland, owing to a cut made in the sixteenth century which diverted the river to its more direct route to the sea below Castle Hill, resulting in the development of 'New Haven'.

Castle Hill and Peacehaven cliffs viewed from above Bishopstone

The walk: 4 miles

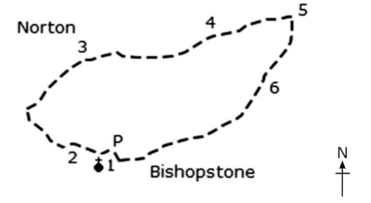

Norton

Bishopstone

N

OS Explorer Map: 123 Eastbourne & Beachy Head

Start: Small parking area near Rookery Cottages in Bishopstone, TQ473001/BN25 2TD

Getting there: Via the A259 one mile west of Seaford

1) Just beyond the parking area at the foot of the hill below Bishopstone church, take a track signed 'The Rookery ¼ mile'. Continue straight ahead at a junction, soon passing over a stile on the right into a field. Follow a narrow, clearly defined track leading diagonally left into the opposite corner and go through a kissing gate, passing through a small patch of rough grassland to join a cross path reached via another kissing gate. Turn right and climb uphill through woodland, finally emerging onto open downland.

2) Take a left fork to reach the top of a rise. Follow the fence line and, at a footpath junction, turn right to join a chalk track leading downhill towards the hamlet of Norton, with Seaford Head just visible away to the right.

3) In the foot of the valley, cross a lane and continue directly ahead onto a track. At the end of this, go through a kissing gate and fork right over a stile beside a field gate. A grass track bears round to the left, passing below a row of low trees and along sloping grassland between two fenced fields.

4) Eventually the track reaches a stile leading onto a narrow enclosed footpath which soon skirts the edge of, and then cuts across the centre of, a large arable field. As the way rises it is worth pausing and looking back towards Newhaven Harbour,

Looking towards Newhaven from Rookery Hill

Castle Hill and the line of the coast as far as Saltdean and Rottingdean.

5) After the path dips over the hill, cross a stile to join a cross track and turn right. Almost immediately, take a fork leading to the right - beside a helpfully located seat - along a path lined with hedge and gorse. Shortly before reaching a concrete track, turn right through a large gap in the hedge to the right and walk along the left hand edge of two fields with the Newhaven coastline visible directly ahead.

6) At the corner of the second field, where a gap in the hedge to the left reveals a glimpse of the covered Blatchington Reservoirs, take a right fork and follow the path downhill, keeping alongside the line of a fence on the left. Pass through a kissing gate at the end of this and, after a few paces, head left between hedgerows to follow the top edge of a steeply sloping field. Shortly before the end of the field, the path curves left and over a stile to meet a track on a bend. Turn right downhill to emerge by a lane opposite the church at Bishopstone; a further right turn downhill completes our circle.

View southeast towards Bishopstone

ONE of the furthest inland in this collection, this route is included for its expansive views over Cuckmere Haven and Newhaven. By stepping back from the coastline it is possible to in one glance appreciate the difference between the Cuckmere and Ouse estuaries – the former an undeveloped Site of Special Scientific Interest, the latter an industrial hub home to an international ferry terminal.

Alfriston also marks our first meeting with the South Downs Way, the 100 mile long distance footpath whose western end lies at Winchester in Hampshire. Two of our next three walks lie almost exclusively along the South Downs Way, but it is hoped that this walk will also prompt an exploration westwards, where vantage points such as Ditchling Beacon, Devil's Dyke and Chanctonbury Ring offer excellent views over both countryside and coastline.

The village of Alfriston itself, nestled at the foot of the Downs by the River Cuckmere, is said to have inspired the hymn 'Morning has Broken', written in 1931 by Eleanor Farjeon.

The River Cuckmere as seen from near High and Over, Alfriston

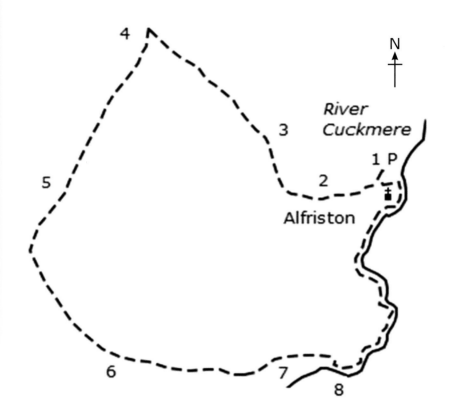

OS Explorer Map: 123: Eastbourne & Beachy Head

Start: The Willows car park off North Street in Alfriston (fee paying), TQ521033/BN26 5UQ

Getting there: Via the A259 or the A27 four miles northeast of Seaford

1) Head into Alfriston village. Just after passing The Star Inn, turn right onto Star Lane. At a cross-junction with Weavers Lane, maintain direction onto Kings Ride, following a sign for the South Downs Way.

2) When this bears right onto The Broadway, continue ahead on an unsurfaced track which heads steeply uphill, offering glimpses left towards Cuckmere Haven. Follow the track as it levels out and begins to curve northwards; when it begins to head back round to the left at a footpath junction, take the right hand option to shortly reach a cross track.

3) Head directly opposite, passing through a wooden gate to ascend with a fence line on the right. Follow the path through a large metal gate into the field beyond [signed 'South Downs Way'] and through a further gate to walk with the fence line on the left.

4) On reaching a signpost beside a footpath junction just as the route enters a dip, turn left, signed 'Wealden Walks'. Pass through a gate beside a metal field gate and follow a track heading downhill. From here there is an excellent vista over some ten miles of coastline taking in landmarks such as Cuckmere Haven, Seaford Head and Newhaven Harbour, as well as Peacehaven and Telscombe Cliffs.

Seaford Bay and Newhaven Harbour

Bishopstone - Beachy Head

67

5) In the bottom of the valley, go straight ahead at a fork to climb steeply up an embankment. At the top of this, head through a gate to reach a cross-track by a sheltered seat and a second fork. Taking the left-hand option, follow a hedge-lined path initially beside a golf course.

6) Shortly after passing a sign for Frog Firle, the path forks again. Take the left hand option, still signed 'Wealden Walks', to follow the left hand edge of fenced grassland. Pass through a number of gates, the fourth of which leads the path into woodland, heading downhill to eventually reach a road.

7) Cross with care towards a gate beside a sign marked 'Litlington 1 mile'. With the Cuckmere estuary visible to the right, head downhill and, just after passing through a second gate, briefly double back to reach the bank of the River Cuckmere itself beside a footbridge.

8) Remain on the same side of the river and turn left to follow the riverbank. After passing Alfriston church, turn left beside a white bridge to join a track on a bend. Continue ahead between flint walls, passing the attractive village green and Clergy House (the first property to be purchased by the National Trust, in 1896) to reach the High Street. Turn right to return to the start.

Alfriston Clergy House and St Andrew's Church

Seaford Head

U NUSUAL among the rivers which dissect the Sussex coastline, the Cuckmere has no harbour, its waters meeting the sea beneath the imposing cliffs of the Seven Sisters and Seaford Head.

A few hundred years ago the area was a shallow tidal estuary; in 1847 the river was straightened, reclaiming pasture and leaving the meanders isolated. Today the area is rich in wildlife and is protected against river and tidal flooding by a shingle beach and earth embankments.

Owing to its lack of development, the area was popular with smugglers dealing in contraband; in response to this, the iconic coastguards' cottages were built in the early nineteenth century and now offer a focus to one of the most recognisable views in Sussex.

On Seaford Head, its defensive role is evidenced in the form of concrete tank tracks laid during WWII. Just west of our start point are also earthen banks marking the remains of an Iron Age hill fort and an earlier Bronze Age barrow.

Coastguards' cottages on Seaford Head

The walk: 3.5 miles

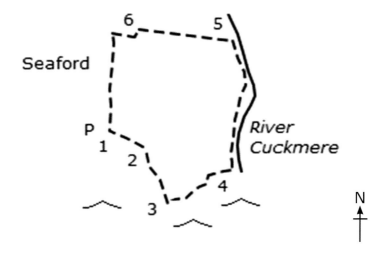

Seaford

River Cuckmere

N

OS Explorer Map: 123 Eastbourne & Beachy Head

Start: Car park at South Hill Barn, TV504981/BN21 4JS

Getting there: From the centre of Seaford, follow Steyne Road, Chyngton Road and Chyngton Way

1) To the left of South Barn, pass a sign for Seaford Head Local Nature Reserve – in whose 250 acres over 200 species of bird have been recorded. At a fork beside a second sign, take the central option on an unsurfaced track with Belle Tout lighthouse visible ahead.

The two concrete tracks either side of this fork were laid during WWII to enable tanks to access the cliff top at Seaford Head, a useful surveillance point for protecting against the threat of invasion.

2) Immediately after passing a gate beside a cattle grid, turn right to pass a bench and head downhill on a grassy track through a short valley opening out above Hope Gap.

This dry valley would once have held a river that is likely to have linked with the River Cuckmere; today, steps allow the opportunity to descend to the current level of the beach, from which there is an excellent view of the line of the Seven Sisters cliffs.

3) Turn left and briefly climb steeply. Follow the cliff edge, passing a number of benches with views towards the Seven Sisters to eventually curve back round to rejoin the unsurfaced track walked earlier just uphill of a handful of coastguards' cottages.

The Seven Sisters viewed from Hope Gap

Bishopstone - Beachy Head

71

This oft-photographed view has appeared in many a film and television programme as an idyllic scene; the coastguards' cottages were built, however, in response to the smuggling that was rife on the uninhabited shores of Cuckmere Haven.

4) Turn right and follow the track downhill to the beach at Cuckmere Haven. On the left lies a memorial to the Canadian troops who were camped here during WWII. Continue ahead to reach the mouth of the river and then turn left to walk inland along the river bank.

5) Eventually this bears left to reach a cross path with views down the wide valley. Go straight ahead through a gate, heading away from the river path which leads to Exceat Bridge and the Golden Galleon pub. Follow the right hand edge of two fields; a gate eventually leads the path round to the left.

6) Very shortly after this, take a right turn on a wide path between fences that emerges opposite Greenholm. Turn left on an unsurfaced lane to pass a few houses and, at a junction, continue ahead on a concrete track. This leads uphill back to Seaford Head and South Barn, offering good views towards Seaford Bay and Newhaven.

Fields by the banks of the River Cuckmere

O N the clifftops of the Seven Sisters, the South Downs Way enjoys its most popular stretch, with thousands of walkers traversing the undulating peaks between Birling Gap and Cuckmere Haven every year.

Our walk begins in the village of East Dean, striking out towards the sea, joining the route of the South Downs Way just west of the coastal hamlet of Birling Gap directly ahead. Walking across all seven of the peaks, we enter the area of chalk downland managed as part of the 690 acres comprising the Seven Sisters Country Park.

Bearing inland along the eastern edge of the Cuckmere Valley, the sight of pillboxes reveals the necessity for wartime defence in this uninhabited stretch of coastline; an airfield was also located near the cliffs in the early 1940s.

The return journey is via Friston Forest and Westdean, where it is believed that King Alfred the Great may have had a palace at a time when tidal flooding would have allowed ships to sail up the valley as far as Exceat.

The Seven Sisters

The walk: 8 miles

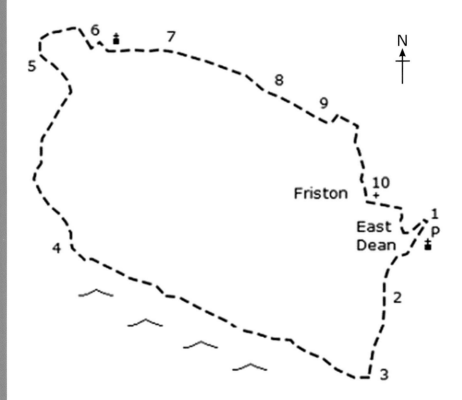

OS Explorer Map: 123 Eastbourne & Beachy Head

Start: Car park at East Dean, TV558978/BN20 0DA

Getting there: Via the A259 four miles west of Eastbourne, following the signs for Birling Gap and Village Green

1) Walk uphill from the car park, passing the Tiger Inn. Turn left across the village green - to the right, a plaque on the wall of a cottage claims that fictional detective Sherlock Holmes retired here. On the far side, meet a residential road. Turn left and, at the fork, take the upper branch onto Went Way. At the end of this, go through a large metal field gate and follow a path which curves left uphill through woodland, signed towards Crowlink.

2) At the top of the hill - the first of the seven 'sisters' - the path emerges onto farmland. Maintain direction, heading to the right of a distinctive orange-roofed barn. Soon the path joins a wide sunken grass track which heads downhill, with Birling Gap and Belle Tout lighthouse visible to the left. Continue through a wooden gate and then through a second gate beside a white weatherboarded cottage onto a chalk track. Very shortly after this, turn right through a kissing gate to join the South Downs Way.

3) Follow the undulating path across the peaks of the Seven Sisters. At one time, these continually eroded cliffs would have held rivers; today they are steep sided dry valleys recognisable nationwide. From East to West, our route crosses Went Hill Brow, Baily's Hill, Flat Hill, Flagstaff Brow, Brass Point, Rough Brow, Short Brow and, finally, Haven Brow.

Seaford Head and the mouth of the River Cuckmere

Bishopstone - Beachy Head

On the seabed below the cliffs lie the remains of a number of shipwrecks - and also that of a U-Boat - some driven ashore by smugglers, some simply washed ashore by inclement weather and dangerous waters.

4) Above the Cuckmere Haven estuary, maintain direction, away from the South Downs Way, to descend towards the valley floor. Cross a stile and curve right towards a kissing gate, passing a pillbox and through a gate to join a path along the foot of the valley. Continue ahead to reach the A259 opposite Seven Sisters Country Park Visitor Centre.

During WWII, the undeveloped Cuckmere Valley was felt likely to be a prime target for invasion, and so was heavily protected by pillboxes, land mines and tank traps; between 1942 and 1946 there was also an airfield, RAF Friston, behind the cliff tops near the Cuckmere Estuary.

5) Turn left to walk along the pavement beside the road for a few paces to reach a bend by a sign for West Dean and Litlington. Cross with care and, immediately to the right of a small road, follow a footpath signed towards Westdean. This passes through the Seven Sisters Country Park car park before entering Friston Forest. Keep to the main bridleway as it begins to curve round to the right, eventually emerging

Cuckmere Haven as seen from Haven Brow

next to a pond in Westdean.

It has been suggested that the secluded hamlet of Westdean was home to the royal estate of Saxon King Alfred the Great. The Old Parsonage in the village, built in the late thirteenth century, is believed to be one of the oldest continually inhabited dwellings in the country.

6) On reaching a cross track in front of Pond Cottage, turn left along a lane - briefly rejoining the South Downs Way on its way to Alfriston. When the South Downs Way soon continues uphill, follow the lane round to the right to pass The Old Parsonage and Church. As the lane begins to bear right again, by Manor Cottage, turn left onto a half-made road, which soon develops into a stony track signed towards Jevington and Friston.

7) Shortly after passing a house on the left, the track forks. Take the right hand option, on a broad bridleway heading uphill. When this finally slopes back downhill and begins to curve left, continue straight ahead on a smaller track.

8) Maintain direction on reaching a cross track, heading uphill to eventually reach the open meadowland of Friston Hill; in the distance, a water tower is visible. Follow the right hand

The Old Parsonage, Westdean

Bishopstone - Beachy Head

77

edge of the meadowland and, on the far side, descend to meet a narrow lane.

9) Turn left, following the course of the lane as it bears right and uphill. By a fingerpost signed towards Friston & East Dean, turn right up a few steps and go through a gate in a wall surrounding parkland. Walk directly across the parkland to a kissing gate in the wall on the far side; beyond this, steps lead down onto the drive to Friston Place. Cross the drive and enter a sloping meadow, heading diagonally left to the top corner where a stile leads the path through a small patch of woodland to reach a road junction beside the A259.

10) Cross the main road with care, passing a pond, then turn left through a Tapsel gate to enter a churchyard. Walk through this, leaving by a second gate into a sloping meadow and heading downhill to reach a lane in East Dean. Bear right to follow the lane back to the village green.

Tapsel gates, thought to be unique to Sussex, are wooden gates which are rotated about a central pivot. Named after a Sussex family, only six examples of the gate are believed to survive; including one in Friston and one in East Dean.

Village green, East Dean

Beachy Head

T HE earliest recording of Beachy Head is as 'Beauchef', its current name being a corruption of the French term meaning 'beautiful headland'. Today, this beautiful headland is one of the most recognisable icons in Sussex, with its high chalk cliff featuring in many a film and television programme.

Our walk takes in the view from the summit - the most southerly point in Sussex after Selsey Bill - and heads westwards in the direction of Belle Tout lighthouse. Confusingly, 'Tout' in this instance derives not from the French, but from the Old English for 'lookout'.

The return is along a ridge of downland behind Beachy Head, briefly joining the South Downs Way as the latter climbs up from its start point on the seafront in Eastbourne.

Line of cliffs from Beachy Head towards Seaford Head

The walk: 5.5 miles

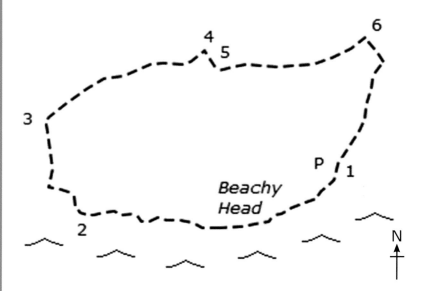

OS Explorer Map: 123 Eastbourne & Beachy Head

Start: Car park at Beachy Head Countryside Centre (fee paying), TV591959/BN20 7YA

Getting there: Via the A259 one mile west of Eastbourne, following the sign for Beachy Head

1) Leaving the car park, cross opposite onto a path signed 'Peace Path'. Follow this surfaced route round to the right, soon emerging onto grassland as it nears Beachy Head itself. After passing Beachy Head, the way begins to undulate steeply.

Rising 530 feet above sea level, Beachy Head is the highest chalk sea cliff in England. On a clear day there are views eastwards over Pevensey Levels towards Hastings and westwards towards Selsey Bill.

2) When the way meets a bend in a road by a parking area and signboard for Belle Tout lighthouse, follow the path beside the edge of the road for a few yards. Almost immediately below Belle Tout lighthouse, cross the road to join a wide concrete track signed towards East Dean Down.

Belle Tout lighthouse was built in 1834 to warn ships of the dangerous cliffs below; however, it was too frequently hidden by mist and so was replaced by the shore-level lighthouse in 1902. In 1999 it was moved 56 feet inland to prevent it being lost to erosion.

3) Follow the track as it passes through Cornish Farm, heading through a wooden gate to the left of a larger metal

Belle Tout lighthouse

field gate to continue on an unsurfaced track to the left of barns. Maintain direction to pass a pumping station.

4) At the end of the track, head through a wooden gate to the right of a larger metal field gate and turn immediately right up a steeply sloping field. At the top of the field, cross over a stile and continue uphill.

5) On reaching the top of the hill, turn left along a grassy track to soon pass a field enclosed by low flint walls. In the South, Beachy Head Visitor Centre and Belle Tout are visible. When the track emerges by a road, cross immediately opposite with care to follow a wide green lane downhill.

6) When this joins a cross track, turn right to pass uphill of a small woodland and follow the signs towards Birling Gap to return to the start point.

Looking towards Eastbourne from Beachy Head

Pevensey Levels - Camber Sands

After the run of the South Downs ends by Eastbourne, the landscape changes dramatically. Chalk cliffs give way to the flat marshland of Pevensey Levels, which at one time would have been a tidal estuary. Beyond, the soils of the High Weald reach the coastline at Bexhill, giving rise to the distinctive sandstone cliffs at Hastings which make such a contrast to those between Brighton and Eastbourne.

Our first walk begins in Hooe, exploring the fertile water meadows of **Pevensey Levels** which, due to a combination of changing sea levels and the build up of shingle beaches caused by longshore drift, have replaced this former tidal saltmarsh. Place names such as Northeye, Pevensey and, further afield, Rye, give clues as to their former situation: the Old English 'ey'- denoting an island.

Owing to its geography, this area has been felt continually prone to attack: the Romans had built a fort on the site of Pevensey Castle as early as the late third century and in the early nineteenth century, 25 Martello towers were built between Eastbourne and Hastings to protect against the

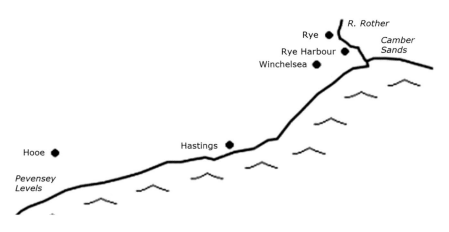

Coastline from Pevensey Levels to Camber Sands

threat of Napoleonic invasion - the highest such concentration in the south of England. In addition to this latter threat, the Royal Military Canal - which we visit near Winchelsea - was built between Pett Level and Seabrook.

It is the Norman invasion, however, for which this stretch of coastline is most famous. William II of Normandy would successfully land here in 1066, constructing his own fortresses at Pevensey and on Castle Hill in Hastings before defeating the Saxons some six miles to the north.

At **Hastings**, the most westerly of the Cinque Ports established to supply ships for the monarchy in times of need, we explore a fertile landscape of slumped hillsides and steep, wooded gullies. The cliffs here, formed by the soft reddy-brown clays and sandstone of the High Weald, are continually eroded by both the sea and valley streams.

Storms in the thirteenth century deeply impacted the town and destroyed the original site of nearby **Winchelsea**. The new town was relocated to a hilltop position a few miles to the north; today, silting and a receding shoreline has caused it to lie stranded inland. The same events resulted in the initial creation of **Rye Harbour** and the later isolation of Camber Castle, both of which we visit before ending our coastal journey in Sussex at **Camber Sands**.

Behind the dunes of Camber Sands

Pevensey Levels

B EGINNING in Hooe, situated on a ridge of land that would once have stood above flooded marsh, this walk initially provides us with excellent views towards the western South Downs as they rise above Eastbourne and stretch northwards to Combe Hill above Polegate.

Striking out into the low-lying Pevensey Levels, our route then explores the patchwork of grazing meadows separated by a network of drainage ditches. This habitat is an important haven for wildlife, with warblers nesting in the reeds and lapwings and snipe wintering in the area.

Much of this marshland lies below high tide level and is today protected by the shingle beach between Pevensey and Cooden. An embankment at the southernmost point of our walk, marking the site of an ancient island settlement, recalls the former intertidal nature of this landscape.

Our return to Hooe offers a view over the expanse of coastline between Pevensey and Cooden, the place where the Normans first left their influential mark on England.

Pevensey Levels with Eastbourne downland beyond

The walk: 4.75 miles

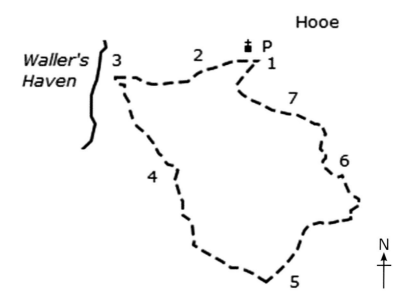

Hooe

Waller's Haven

3 2 P 1 7 6 4 5

N

OS Explorer Map: 124 Hastings & Bexhill

Start: Parking area by St Oswald's Church in Hooe, TQ683092/TN33 9HT

Getting there: Via the A259 four miles northeast of Pevensey, following the B2095 towards Battle and then the sign for Hooe Church

1) Follow the path in front of Hooe church, where one path leads downhill through thin woodland. Ignore this and skirt right around the edge of the churchyard; ahead, leave the churchyard through a kissing gate labelled 'Wealden Walks'. Follow the left hand edge of a field and shortly pass into a second, continuing uphill along its left hand edge to diverge from the route of Wealden Walks. In the top corner, head through a gap in the hedgerow and maintain direction between trees. A gate by Grove House leads the path onto a lane beside the road to Hooe Common.

2) Turn left along this larger road, soon continuing ahead onto Horsewalk as the main road veers away to the left. This is a narrow tarmac road which leads westwards downhill to Horse Bridge. On the left, excellent glimpses of the coastline can be seen while, straight ahead, the South Downs rise imposingly.

3) Immediately before reaching the bridge over a waterway, turn left to walk a few paces along the edge of the riverbank. Pass through a gate next to a sign for Pike Anglers Club. Cross a stile and turn immediately left, then very shortly cross a second stile next to a farm gate and turn immediately right. At this point the route heads out into Pevensey Levels, a designated Site of Special Scientific Interest. Follow the

View from Horsewalk

Pevensey Levels - Camber Sands

line of telegraph poles through a field to reach another stile by a farm gate. Cross this and follow the edge of Waterford Stream, which is made visible by the reeds on the left. Maintain direction over a further stile and cross this onto a lane, turning left to reach The Lamb pub. Turn right to reach the busy A259.

4) Cross this with extreme care and turn right. A few yards away, immediately before a stone bridge, turn left over a stile by a rusty gate (again signed 'Wealden Walks'). Follow the line of a channel, and continue to follow this as it bears right shortly after the path passes through a metal gate. Soon the route is directed left and over a stile; bear right after this to skirt the right hand side of a field. Maintaining direction, cross a channel and head through the centre of a further field to a fingerpost (over another channel). A stile on the right by a farm gate keeps the direction heading left. Follow the channel on the left hand side, eventually crossing a wide wooden slatted bridge to reach a junction.

Earthworks on the right are all that remains of the ancient village of Northeye, once a thriving community on an island amidst mostly flooded marshland. Possessing a chapel and manor, it was significant enough to be one of the subsidiaries of the Cinque Port of Hastings. Storms and changes in sea

Normans Bay

level meant the village had been completely abandoned by the seventeenth century.

5) Continue straight ahead, following the track as it soon starts to head uphill. When the track joins a lane, turn right; from here there are good views southwards to Normans Bay. Follow the lane to the main road and cross this with care, heading immediately opposite over a stile by a farm gate. Follow the left hand edge of the field beyond to climb briefly uphill, with the view behind reaching across to Cooden. Soon a track leads downhill, with a hedgerow on the right, the wide expanse of the Downs in the distance to the left and the church at Hooe visible straight ahead.

6) At the foot of the hill, cross a drainage channel and turn left. Follow the line of the channel on the left and head shortly over a stile by a metal gate. After passing through a second metal gate, continue straight ahead, again keeping the line of the channel close to the left. In the top left corner of the field beyond, cross another stile by a gate and maintain direction, still following the channel's meandering line. In the top left corner of this next field, the channel meets a second running perpendicular to it and the route is guided left around the edge of a new reedbank project. Very soon the way leads right, crossing this second channel to head uphill along the

Looking towards Cooden

Pevensey Levels - Camber Sands

left hand edge of a hedge-lined field. Maintain direction as the path skirts the edge of a house to emerge onto a lane.

7) Cross over this onto Kiln Lane, passing Court Lodge. Soon there are views over the coast to the left, with Hooe church not far away on the right. Just by a sign for Burresgroves, turn right onto a gravel track which soon turns into a concrete drive. Cross two stiles in quick succession and follow the left hand edge of a field downhill to re-emerge in the churchyard.

St Oswald's Church, Hooe

I N Hastings, the sandstone of the High Weald reaches the coast, supporting heathland and woodland as far as the cliff edge. Here, Pre-Raphaelite artist William Holman Hunt found inspiration for painting 'Our English Coasts, 1852 ("Strayed Sheep")'; another Pre-Raphaelite, Dante Gabriel Rossetti, was a frequent visitor to Hastings and married his wife in St Clement's Church.

The walk begins on The Stade, believed to be home to Europe's largest beach-launched fishing fleet. We climb East Hill - either on foot or by cliff railway - from which it is possible to appreciate the town's valley location.

Our route also quickly moves into a landscape of steep sided wooded valleys carved out of the soft sandstone by streams. We cross two of these, with the option to extend the walk through a third to reach the top of the Firehills to enjoy an excellent view across to Romney Marsh. This adds 1.25 miles to the trip.

The Downs at Eastbourne as seen from the cliffs at Hastings

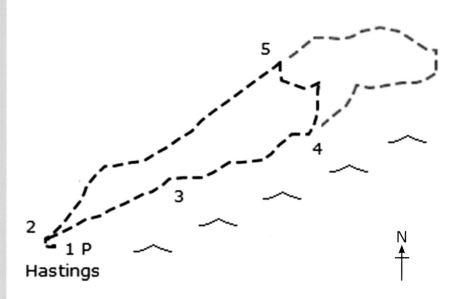

OS Explorer Map: 124 Hastings & Bexhill

Start: Car park at Rock-A-Nore (fee-paying), TQ830096/ TN34 3DW

Getting there: Via the A259, following signs for Jerwood Gallery and Rock-A-Nore

1) Leaving the car park, walk back along the road by The Stade, a shingle beach which is home to Europe's largest fleet of beach-launched fishing boats.

'Stade' is an old Saxon word meaning 'landing place'. The tall black wooden sheds are net shops, built to provide a weatherproof store for fishing gear; the first of these was erected in 1834 shortly after the completion of the first of the town's groynes, which created a very limited beach area on which to build – hence the buildings' height.

On the right is the East Hill Lift, a cliff railway - currently the steepest in the UK - which climbs a little over 265 feet to reach the top of East Hill. For those wishing to walk, continue ahead and, immediately after passing The Dolphin pub, turn right up Tamarisk Steps. At a junction, follow the sign right to East Hill. Emerging at the end of a lane, turn right and follow a further flight of steps to reach Hastings Country Park and the top station of the East Hill Lift. From here there are excellent views over Hastings, Bexhill and back towards Beachy Head at Eastbourne. This point also marks the westernmost extent of the Saxon Shore Way, a long-distance footpath which traces the line of the coast between Hastings and Gravesend in Kent as it would have been some 1500 years ago.

East Hill Lift, Hastings

2) Turn right: signed 'Scenic Walks, Glens and Firehills'. Keeping to the right of a beacon, climb uphill; once over the brow of the hill, the headland at Dungeness is visible. Keep right and follow the line of the cliff, eventually heading into woodland where a sign guides the path downhill via steps into Ecclesbourne Glen.

3) Cross over the steep-sided valley - cut by a narrow stream - and then head up a few steps on the opposite side, now signed towards Fairlight Glen and Firehills. At the top of the hill, a bench allows the opportunity to enjoy the view looking back as far as Eastbourne. Continue along a wide grass path; fenced off on the left is Ecclesbourne meadow restoration project, designed to protect this rare coastal cliff top grassland which is under threat from intensive farming and encroaching scrub. Wheatears, whinchats and meadow pipits can be seen here in summer.

Soon, a path joins from the left as the route descends through woodland into the second valley of Fairlight Glen. At the foot of this, a sign currently reads that, due to recent cliff falls, access to the beach here is closed. Climb uphill out of the glen; the path begins to head inland and soon arrives at a junction. At this point, there is the option to extend the walk by 1.25 miles by heading through a third valley to reach the

Ecclesbourne Glen

top of Firehills.

Short version: 4a) Go straight ahead, continuing inland through Dripping Well and crossing two streams feeding into the gully below. Follow the path round past an information board and then, at a Y-junction, take the right fork: signed 'Barley Lane ½ mile'. A fenced grass track leads through a metal gate and onto a track between hedgerows to reach a T-junction with Barley Lane. On the route, there are views left to Hastings, Eastbourne and the coastline by Normans Bay and Pevensey Levels. Upon reaching Barley Lane, turn left: signed 'East Hill 1¼ miles'.

Long version: 4b) Turn right, continuing to follow the sign towards Firehills, and climb the steps to the top of the cliff, shortly to descend again into Warren Glen. Ignore a left turn and cross over another stream in a gully. Ascending the other side, turn right – still signed towards Firehills. At the top of the climb, beneath a beacon, turn left up towards a lane beside coastguards' cottages. A little way ahead is Fairlight Visitor Centre. Immediately beyond the coastguards' cottages turn left and shortly head through a gate. Follow a sign for Barley Lane onto a track between fences with the sea on the left. At a junction, follow a path left through a pair of kissing gates, again signed towards Barley Lane. On reaching a cross

View towards Dungeness from coastguards' cottages above Firehills

junction, go straight ahead through another kissing gate, first along a fenced grass track and then on a narrow hedge-lined path - which can be muddy in winter - to eventually emerge via a final kissing gate onto a lane. Maintain direction onto Barley Lane, on which a fingerpost signifies that this is part of the 1066 Country Walk. Shortly afterwards, a signpost denotes that Hastings is two miles away - with Dover 50 miles behind.

5) Follow the road as it gradually heads downhill. When it eventually forks, bear left. When this road runs out, continue ahead onto a track back into Hastings Country Park. On reaching grassland, turn right and keep to the right hand edge. Soon the beacon passed earlier is visible and aiming directly for this allows the route to rejoin the top station of the East Hill Lift and retrace the opening of the walk back to The Stade and Rock-A-Nore.

Net shops on The Stade

T HE original site of Winchelsea, on a shingle bank, was fully submerged by the sea in the thirteenth century. Due to its importance as a port, it had already been transferred to the more secure location it occupies today, atop a hill beside the River Brede. A combination of harbour silting, plagues and French raids would later deplete the significance of the town, which now lies three miles inland.

We begin by the Church of St Thomas the Martyr, situated within Winchelsea's planned grid-like network of streets. Striking out downhill near New Gate, the former south entrance to the town, the route crosses shallow undulating hillside towards Pett and Cliff End.

The return journey begins with a level stroll beside the Royal Military Canal, which runs 28 miles from Cliff End to Hythe and was completed in 1809 to protect this stretch of coastline from the threat of Napoleonic invasion. Finally, there is a brief ascent to reach Landgate, the northeastern entrance to this once thriving port.

View from Strand Gate, Winchelsea

The walk: 8 miles

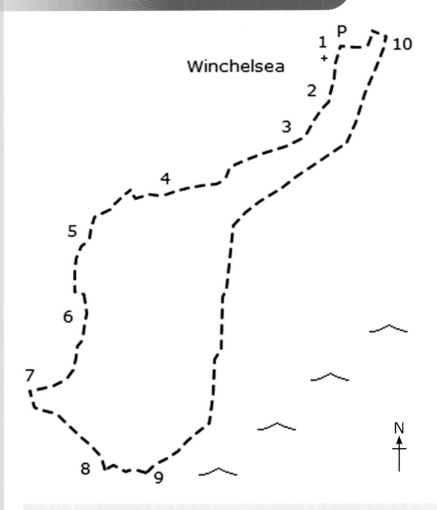

Winchelsea

OS Explorer Map: 124 Hastings & Bexhill

Start: High Street in Winchelsea, TQ905173/TN36 4EB

Getting there: Via the A259 three miles west of Rye

1) Bear left by the New Inn pub onto German Street, passing St Thomas's Church on the left; in the churchyard, Spike Milligan is buried. Pass Wesley's Tree – so-called since John Wesley preached his last open air sermon here in 1790 - and continue onto Monks Walk. When this bears right, cross opposite over a low stone wall to the right of a large isolated section of flint wall: the only visible remains of four almshouses for the poor once located in the town.

2) Strike half right downhill, joining the route of the 1066 Country Walk, across a number of mounds and dips which are all that remains of the suburbs of the medieval town which was abandoned by the fifteenth century as the port began to silt up. Cross over two stiles in quick succession and continue half right downhill, passing to the left of a small clump of trees and over a stile to the left of a wooden gate. On the left is New Gate, the southernmost boundary of the original town. The Town Ditch, the former defensive moat surrounding the town, can also be seen.

3) Head straight uphill through the centre of a field to the left of the sixteenth century buildings of Wickham Manor Farm: once owned by William Penn, founder of Pennsylvania. Go over a stile immediately to the left of a farm house and cross a track. A stile leads the route directly ahead through the centre of the next field and along the left hand side of

St Thomas's Church, Winchelsea

Pevensey Levels - Camber Sands

the field beyond: signed towards Icklesham. Very shortly the route bears left across a lane and through a gate into a field. Head diagonally right over the brow of a hill to a stile by a double gate to the left of the fence line. Following the right hand field edge, cross two stiles in quick succession onto a clear path through rough grassland which reaches a lane.

4) Continue ahead on the lane, passing below a windmill; the 1066 Country Walk veers away above this. The windmill is Hog Hill Mill, now owned by Sir Paul McCartney as a private recording studio. On reaching a fork in the lane, turn right and almost immediately left through a kissing gate. The route has been diverted right along the side of a large building, turning left onto a track which soon becomes rough grass between fences. Follow this through a large metal gate and maintain direction straight ahead when joined by another path on the right. Follow the route of a lane on the left and, just before the path bears round to the right, descend six steep steps to join it.

5) Maintain direction along the lane, crossing a small bridge. When the road bears round to the right by the entrance to Pannel Farm, turn left through a large metal field gate. Follow the left hand field edge and, shortly after passing farm buildings on the left, turn left over a stile to the right of a metal field gate. Continue ahead to another stile by a field

Pett Level as seen from Wickham Manor Farm

gate at the top of the hill.

6) Go directly ahead over the brow over the hill, descending towards a small wooden bridge over a stream. Climb the left hand side of the field beyond. Turn through a large metal gate and bear right onto a lane. Follow this until it reaches the Royal Oak pub by Pett Road.

7) Turn left to pass Pett Recreation Ground. After 500 yards, immediately opposite a house called Jacques, turn right up a track and over a stile marking this as the route of the Maritime Heritage Trail. Cross the centre of the field beyond to a second clearly visible stile, heading diagonally right down the hill and over a third stile which leads again downhill to cross a small bridge over a stream. Head directly ahead through a brief patch of tussocky grass and over a second bridge to reach a farmhouse.

8) Turn left over a new stile by a wooden gate and walk along the left hand edge of the field beyond. Shortly after passing a white walled building, turn left over a stile by a wooden fence to reach a lane.

9) Turn left, passing a junction leading back towards Pett to reach a canal opposite a limited-time parking area. Turn left onto the Royal Military Canal Path to walk along the north side

The Royal Military Canal

of the canal. Maintain direction on reaching the first bridge, heading through a low wooden gate; this briefly turns away from the canal onto rough grassland to reach a cliff on which is a surveillance tower. Turn right to reach a second bridge, this time crossing it to continue along the southern edge of the canal. From here, the canal leads the path inland for some three miles. The levels to the right are protected as part of the Dungeness, Romney Marsh and Rye Bay Site of Special Scientific Interest.

The lefthand view is akin to the backdrop of Pre-Raphaelite artist Sir John Everett Millais's 'The Blind Girl', painted here in 1855. The town also featured in William Makepeace Thackeray's unfinished novel 'Denis Duval'; another writer, Ford Maddox Ford, lived in Winchelsea between 1901 and 1907 with Joseph Conrad also renting here.

10) On eventually reaching a road by Winchelsea, turn left back over the canal to meet the A259. Briefly maintain direction straight ahead, soon turning left to climb steeply uphill to Strand Gate, a flint fortification built in the early fourteenth century to defend the port of Winchelsea. Today, a bench here offers excellent views towards Rye, Romney Marsh and Camber. Follow the road as it bears right into Winchelsea to return to the High Street.

Town sign in Winchelsea

Rye Harbour

THE storms in the thirteenth century which so greatly affected Winchelsea also diverted the original course of the River Rother some 15 miles westwards to enter the sea at its current location of Rye. This enabled Rye to develop as a thriving port, but when the sea later retreated, its effectiveness was reduced - as was the case at Winchelsea.

Our walk begins two miles south of Rye, in the village of Rye Harbour, beside the final Martello tower to be located in Sussex - which itself now lies just under a mile inland. Following the River Rother southwards to the sea, we then turns westwards beside the beach before heading inland across an area of open shingle and saltmarsh. This area is a designated Site of Special Scientific Interest, part of which forms a local nature reserve, and is an important habitat for flora and fauna, including little terns.

On our return to Rye Harbour we pass the ruins of Camber Castle, a fortification once situated on a spit of land protecting the estuary, but now lying isolated amidst fields.

Looking towards Fairlight cliffs

The walk: 5.75 miles

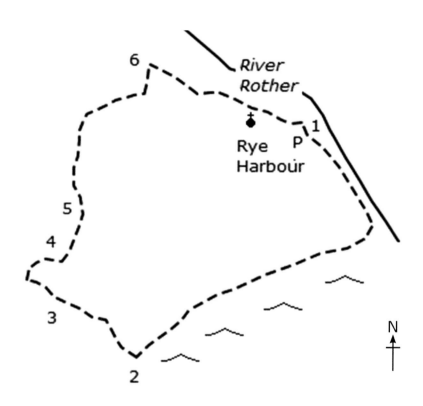

River Rother

Rye Harbour

P

N

OS Explorer Map: 125 Romney Marsh

Start: Car park at Rye Harbour, TQ942188/TN13 7TU

Getting there: Via the A259 in Rye, following Harbour Road south beside the river Brede

1) Turn right upon leaving the car park to follow a private road between the river and saltmarsh signed 'Rye Harbour Nature Reserve'. Just before reaching the harbour mouth, turn right onto a tarmac road used by the Environment Agency. At this point it is possible to detour to the beach, with Fairlight cliffs visible ahead and Camber Sands behind.

2) Just beyond the old lifeboat house, at a zebra crossing beside a nature reserve sign, turn right away from the road. Head along a raised path between fields; at a cross junction, continue ahead to pass a large pool on the right. The path soon goes through woodland and across a bridge over a ditch to reach a staggered junction by a driveway.

3) Cross a stile and continue straight ahead through a small field and over a narrow wooden bridge. A sign just beyond this directs the route along the left hand side of the field beyond, through a gate and along the left hand side of a further field. Cross another wooden bridge, and then a stile, to join a lane. Turn right.

4) Follow the lane round to the right as it becomes a gravel driveway passing farm buildings. At a fork, turn left beside a sign marking this as the route of the Saxon Shore Way. Keep a fence close to the right and follow the track as it passes a small clump of trees and then sweeps left.

Mary Stanford lifeboat house

5) When a broad expanse of shingle comes into view, look for a pathway on the left between hedges; a map of footpaths on the right-hand fence line at this point confirms this as the correct location. Turn left; the broad expanse of Castle Water is immediately to the right. Keep Castle Water as close to the right as possible, following grassy tracks that eventually reach a small metal gate; a bird hide is accessible through a wooden gate to the right. Turn left and walk straight ahead towards Camber Castle.

Camber Castle was built in the early sixteenth century to guard Rye, but, after already having its tower raised once, was finally officially abandoned in 1637 after silting and the gradual retreat of the sea rendered it ineffective.

Just beyond the castle, the route joins a grassy cross track running left to right. Turn right and walk towards an isolated willow tree. Go through a wooden gate beside the tree and follow the right hand fence line. At a second gate, follow the left hand fence line to a third gate and follow the path as it bears left through a nature reserve.

6) Just before reaching a wooden bridge, turn right. Warehouse buildings are visible beyond the trees to the left. As the path widens, keep to the left to be guided to Harbour Road. Turn right to return to Rye Harbour village.

Camber Castle

Rye/Camber Sands

PERCHED atop a hill, with its church visible for some distance, Rye's name is thought to derive, like the place names of Pevensey and Northeye mentioned previously, from its one-time situation as an island.

Beginning in the town itself, our walk heads through Rye's cobbled streets, passing the home of author Henry James and the strategically located St Mary's Church.

Descending to cross the River Rother, we then strike out into the western part of Romney Marsh with its low-lying grazing land and network of drainage channels. Like the routes at Rye Harbour and Winchelsea, this walk lies within the 22,000 acres of biologically and geologically important habitats covered by the Dungeness, Romney Marsh and Rye Bay Site of Special Scientific Interest.

Leaving the Marsh, we emerge onto the broad expanse of Camber Sands, the only sand dune system in East Sussex and famed the country over. Finally, we leave Camber Sands to follow the banks of the River Rother back to Rye.

Camber Sands

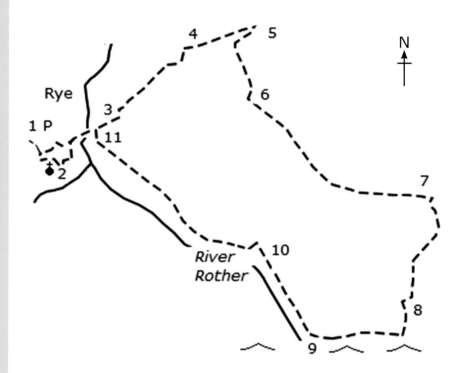

OS Explorer Map: 125 Romney Marsh

Start: Car park at Rye Station (fee paying), TQ920206/ TN31 7AB

Getting there: Via the A259, following signs for Rye town centre and Rye station

1) Head uphill from the station and cross the main road beside the Cinque Ports pub. Continue uphill onto Market Road, passing Jempson's café. At a T-junction with the High Street, turn right and then almost immediately left up the cobbled West Street, which soon bears left after passing Lamb House – the one-time home of Henry James. Follow the alleyway round to the left of St Mary's Church to pass the North Door, from which there is (fee paying) access to the tower. Beyond this, bear right round the side of the church and continue ahead over Church Square towards Ypres Tower and Gun Garden.

2) Pass through the Gun Garden and head down the steps beside Ypres Castle Inn to reach the A259. Cross with care onto Rock Channel and bear left, following the tarmac path beside the Town Salts. On reaching the A259 for a second time, cross with care and turn right over the River Rother.

3) Follow the pavement beside the A259 to cross Kings Avenue. On meeting this for a second time a few hundred yards later, turn left along it and then very shortly right onto a footpath signed towards East Guldeford. This briefly passes between houses and then strikes out across a narrow strip of rough grassland. On the far side, pass through a metal gate and maintain direction through the grassland beyond.

St Mary's Church, Rye

Pevensey Levels - Camber Sands

109

At the end of this, head through a second metal gate and turn immediately left along an embankment towards a stile in front of a house. Turn right down its drive to reach the main road.

4) Cross immediately opposite onto a track beside Half Acre Farm and through a large metal field gate. Maintain direction across a small patch of rough grassland to a second gate, passing a bridge on the right which leads to the isolated church at East Guldeford. Continue ahead, with a channel on the right, through a further field gate to soon reach a second bridge.

5) Turn right over the bridge, after which an arrow points diagonally right towards a chimneyed house. Here, the route runs through the low-lying, reclaimed marshland of East Guldeford Level. Maintain direction to cross a second bridge and continue ahead to an isolated barn at Moneypenny Farm.

6) Pass through a wide metal field gate, turning right and then sharply left around the southern side of the barn to join a gravel track. This shortly passes a lake away to the left, before developing into a grassy track on an embankment which eventually swings left. Maintain direction on this wide grassy track as it briefly dips below the embankment.

East Guldeford Level

7) On reaching a wooden bridge on the left, turn right and bear diagonally left to the corner of a field, aiming directly towards an isolated pillbox. Pass through a metal field gate and maintain direction to reach the pillbox itself. Turn left up the embankment beside this and then very shortly right onto a concrete drive. Head through a metal gate as the drive becomes gravelled before reaching Camber Road.

8) Walk beside a cycle lane on the right for a few yards and then turn left, crossing the road with care to head through a wooden kissing gate. Follow the right hand edge of a grassy car park, soon climbing a sandy embankment to reach the dunes of Camber Sands. Turn right along the beach. At this point, we are now some 14 miles further inland than Sussex's most southerly point, Selsey Bill.

9) On reaching the mouth of the River Rother at Rye Harbour, turn right and head inland, following the edge of the river channel. Soon the route turns right through a gate to follow a path slightly set back from the river edge itself. Just before the Harbour Master building, the path bears right around a house to join a concrete parking area beside a two-tone green outbuilding. On the ground are forking tramlines showing the route of the Rye and Camber Tramway which was operational between 1895 and 1939.

Dunes on Camber Sands

Pevensey Levels - Camber Sands

10) Follow a tarmac lane which runs along this old tramway course and then, when the lane swings round to the right, continue ahead towards a house and bear left to return to the Rother. Follow the riverbank as it heads back towards Rye, passing a private lake, and later a pillbox, on the right. Eventually the path curves round to the right to return to the bridge carrying the A259 over the river.

11) Turn left. Follow the right hand edge of the Town Salts behind a small car park to reach a pedestrian crossing by Rye Bowls Club. Cross the A259 and climb the steps to Hilder's Cliff. On the right is Landgate, the only remaining entrance gate of the four originally built to protect the town. Turn left and follow the road round to the right onto the High Street, at the corner of which is a good view over the coastline and the route just walked. Once on the High Street, the second turning on the right rejoins Market Street and the outward route from Rye station.

Rye from the banks of the River Rother

We hope you have enjoyed this book. S B Publications has numerous titles which cover in further detail many of the areas and places touched on in these pages.

Information on these can be found at:

www.sbpublications.co.uk